Jarrold Wild Flowers Series Book 3
With text by **E. A. Ellis**

# Wild Flowers
# of the Coast

Jarrold Colour Publications, Norwich

**1** × 1·50

**1. SEA PURSLANE** (*Halimione portulacoides*). This low-growing and rather shrubby member of the spinach family forms grey hummocks and long ridges cresting the sides of tidal creeks in salt-marshes. It is most abundant on our east coast. By straining muddy water as it brims over, the plant helps to raise the level of the marshes. The silvery leaves are frosted with scales which reduce loss of moisture in hot weather. Small 'gold-dusted' flowers appear late in summer seen growing here with Common Sea Lavender.

*Figures in red beside each picture show the scale of reproduction.*

At the seaside, perhaps more than anywhere else, we see very clearly how various natural features of the landscape are distinguished by their vegetation. There is a well-defined pattern. In the sea itself, where the water is clear and the shore gently shelving, we may find beds of bright green eel-grass growing just below extreme low-water: a flowering plant that shares the home of seaweeds. We next meet with land plants along the strand line where wrack, rubbish and sea-borne seeds are deposited at the limits of the highest tides. Ephemeral annuals such as the little lilac-flowered sea rocket and prickly saltwort specialise in this way of life. Then the sea couch grass takes hold with matted roots and spear leaves catching and gathering the wind-drifted sands to consolidate the upper beach. This hardy pioneer thrives in the presence of salt and stands up to the friction of blown sand, preparing the way for the more prominent, wiry marram grass which is the chief builder of our sand dunes. Shingle banks and spits are features of many stretches of our coast. Much of the shingle is mobile, being subjected to the action of storm waves from time to time, especially in winter. Certain plants such as the sea pea, sea campion and yellow horned poppy are able to colonise this loose material, anchoring themselves by deep and extensive roots and in this way some stability is achieved. In some cases old shingle beds become cut off from the sea as beaches build up and they then provide a more secure home for a number of other plants such as stonecrops, sea heath, rock sea lavender and shrubby seablite. The massive dunes tufted by marram grass receive their sand from beaches whose sand dries at the surface while the tides are out and is wafted farther inshore by sea breezes, where the tussocky plants arrest its progress. The newest dunes are still yellow where the fresh sand is exposed between the marrams, but soon many of the spaces are filled by sea holly and sea bindweed and a few other plants which thrive where the sand is fresh and contains limy fragments of sea shells and mineral salts from sea water. As the sheltering cover increases and the dead remains of pioneer plants accumulate, mosses and lichens form carpets over the sand and many more kinds of flowering plants appear. With age, the dunes lose their yellow look and in winter appear grey with their covering of bleached and withered vegetation, while in summer they are bright with many dwarf flowers. As time goes on, sheltered valleys in the dunes gather a crust of peat which holds moisture like a sponge. Rain-water dissolves and washes all traces of lime from the surface layer and the hollows are then colonised by heath and bog plants characteristic of acid soils. Where rivers enter the sea there are often large expanses of tidal estuaries where fresh and salt waters mix. Mud brought down by the rivers is deposited as brown and blue clay through the action of salt, so that vast mudflats veined by winding channels are exposed at low tide. In summer the muds which are flooded regularly by tidal waters may often be seen covered with succulent marsh samphire. At slightly higher levels there may be quantities of sea aster, sea lavender or perhaps the coarse Townsend's cord-grass, further building up and consolidating the mud. There is a gradual increase in the variety of plant life with the development of salt-marshes, with certain species selecting the high and well-drained ground reached only occasionally by tidal floods. The plants are different, but there is the same pattern of transition as on more open shores. There are also gradual changes in riverside vegetation upstream to where the effects of salt tides cease to be evident. For instance, the white-flowered scurvy-grass can be found many miles inland where the water is only very faintly brackish. Estuary muds are much enriched by minerals and other plant foods draining into rivers; they also have masses of weedy rubbish washed up along their shores and shell beds formed in some of the bays favour the growth of lime-loving plants.

Many wild flowers found growing on sea cliffs can also be found inland, but some are restricted to the coast, flourishing only within reach of the salt sea spray. They may be lodged on ledges and crests of precipices or cluster mainly on the rocks below, moistened by seeping water from cliff faces as well as by drifting foam. Cliffs of chalk and limestone have their own special plants while granites and the like provide niches for those which avoid lime; but even where the rocks themselves offer little for the nourishment of plant life, the fertile 'whitewash' supplied by countless sea-birds supplies what is needed. The process of soil-building on rock ledges is relatively slow and precarious, but, little by little, decayed vegetable matter and rock sediments accumulate in the crannies and provide for the growth of turf and additional kinds of plants which can only become established after the ground has been prepared in this way. Along many miles of our coastline the cliffs are of soft clay, gravel and sand left behind by melting glaciers in the not very distant past. These cliffs are very unstable and are always crumbling while the sea washes away the material as it falls on to the beaches below. In some places large landslips of clay persist for several years and develop a rich and varied plant life. Elsewhere, the exposure of chalky boulder-clay on an unstable cliff-face may provide a temporary home for unusual plants whose seeds have been introduced by birds. But, on the whole, these cliffs support very few purely coastal types of vegetation.

Plants living near the sea in Britain experience the benefits of a maritime climate. There is a tendency for winter temperatures to be slightly higher on the coast than inland and in summer this is reversed; but the extra winter warmth enjoyed in the south and west is of critical importance for a number of flowers which are unable to survive where freezing winds strike the east coast and the average winter temperature is distinctly lower. It is interesting to find that several species reach their northern European limits of distribution in this country. Many seaside plants are fleshy succulents, storing water in their leaves and losing very little through their specially small pores. In some cases these provisions are made as a consequence of having to function in a salty habitat; in other cases the plants must be able to withstand the heat and drought of burning sand in summer, and in the grasses of sand dunes the leaves conserve their moisture by assuming a cylindrical shape. Dunes are less barren than might be expected from the external appearance of vast masses of hummocky sand. They do in fact collect a lot of water from the moist sea air which is condensed on the surface as the sands cool rapidly at night. Beneath the sandhills one can usually find a layer of fresh water riding on top of the salt water penetrating the depths from the sea.

There is a refreshing wildness about the vegetation of our coast. Its patterns are so clearly the result of natural adaptations to the dynamic environment created by the interaction of sea and land at various levels. We and our flocks and herds have greatly modified the face of the countryside, but the primeval world survives on sea-girt crags, rolling sand dunes and desolate salt flats where the tides ebb and flow in perfect freedom.

In the past, sporadic expansion of seaside towns and holiday camps has destroyed many beautiful features of our coastline; but the National Trust, County Naturalists' Trusts and the Nature Conservancy have been very active recently in saving what has remained unspoiled. More and more people explore the coast for pleasure year by year and take an increasing interest in the birds and flowers; but unrestricted trampling, picnic fires and the thoughtless disposal of litter are having unfortunate effects in the more popular beauty spots. A rich and varied patchwork of wild flowers can only survive for all to enjoy in the future if ramblers refrain from uprooting, picking or otherwise damaging the vegetation.

2 ×1·25
3 ×0·50

**2. GLADDON** (*Iris foetidissima*).
Tufts of the dark sword-leaves of
this iris share cliff slopes with black-
thorn and bramble in the south and
west of England and are found less
commonly elsewhere in open woods
and on hedge-banks, chiefly on light,
limy soils. The rather dull, papery,
brownish-violet flowers have an un-
pleasant smell which attracts small
flies and beetles. They are succeeded
by plump pods which split on ripening to reveal rows of fiery orange
berries. These are fully exposed in
winter and resemble coral beads.

**3. THRIFT** (*Armeria maritima*). Tufts
of these sea pinks often grow in great
profusion on rocky cliffs. They also
carpet the higher levels of salt-
marshes with rosy, honey-scented
blossoms in early summer. After
flowering the papery seed-heads may
persist for some months. Where the
climate is mild, the cushions of finely
grassy leaves remain green almost
throughout the year, but on bleak
coasts they wither in winter and the
plants make slower growth. A long-
stalked variety grows inland on
limestone.

**4. SPRING SQUILL** (*Scilla verna*).
Patches of this vividly coloured minia-
ture bluebell bring enchantment to
grassy cliff slopes in early spring.
These flowers are only very locally
concentrated, chiefly along the rock-
iest parts of our coast, so careful
conservation will be necessary if they
are to survive in busy holiday centres.

**5. DOG VIOLET** (*Viola canina*). This
is the bluest of our wild violets and
may be found in bloom from March
to June. It avoids limy soils and grows
in open, sunny spots, especially on
heaths and coastal sand dunes. Its
closely tufted growth distinguishes it
from other, more spreading violets
found in woods and along hedge-
banks. The ripe seeds are often
collected and stored by ants.

4 × 1·50
5 × 1·50

**6** ×1·50
**7** ×2·00

**6. SLENDER BIRD'S-FOOT TREFOIL** (*Lotus tenuis*). This has longer and more wiry stems than the common kind; its leaves are much narrower and there are seldom more than four blossoms in each cluster. It grows in dry, turfy places or on bare sandy soil, especially near the sea and is often to be seen splashing the banks and walls of estuaries with gold in summer. It is also found in some inland haunts here and there in the south-eastern half of England, but it is not a native of Scotland or Ireland.

**7. BIRD'S-FOOT TREFOIL** (*Lotus corniculatus*). Often called 'Bacon and Eggs', from the rich yellow and reddish streaking of its flowers, this showy little member of the pea family grows on dry, grassy banks all over Britain. Its massed blossoms are often plentiful on sand and shingle along the coast. They have a sweet and delicious fragrance like that of flowering gorse on warm, sunny days. The clusters of long, slender pods have some likeness to the clawed toes of small birds; they curl and split on drying to expel the seeds.

**8. LONG-LEAVED SCURVY-GRASS** (*Cochlearia anglica*). This is the lushest of the several scurvy-grasses producing conspicuous white flowers round the edges of muddy salt-marshes in early spring. Certain of these fleshy-leaved plants are plentiful on remote Arctic islands, where they used to be gathered and eaten by mariners as a protection against scurvy in the days of sailing ships. The species illustrated is common in south and east England, scarcer in the north, and is distinguished by its long, tapering basal leaves.

**8** $\times$ 0·50

**9. SEA PEA** (*Lathyrus japonicus*, spp. *maritimus*). This deep-rooting perennial pea is plentiful on the crests of shingle banks along several parts of the coast, chiefly in East Anglia and the south. The blue-green foliage is visible almost throughout the year and the flowers appear from June to August. Although the seeds are relatively small they have been gathered as food in times of famine. The pods are straight, up to two inches long, and contain from four to eight seeds.

**10. SEA KALE** (*Crambe maritima*). Although only locally common, this large and showy member of the cabbage family is widely distributed round the English coast. It grows mainly on beach shingle at the level reached by the highest tides. A long-lived perennial, it is firmly rooted and can grow up through masses of shingle after it has been buried during winter storms. The large, wavy, cabbage-like leaves are of a blue-green colour. This species is often cultivated as a salad vegetable.

**11. ENGLISH STONECROP** (*Sedum anglicum*). This dwarf rock-plant forms spreading mats and cushions on ledges of sea cliffs and mountains and is often plentiful on sand dunes and beach shingle ridges, especially in the west of Britain. It grows best on acid rocks and avoids chalk and limestone. The fleshy leaves are of a frosty blue-green tint up to the time of flowering and then become tinged with red. The white petals are pinkish underneath and the ripening fruits are scarlet and crimson.

**9** × 1·25

10 × 0·50
11 × 1·50

**12** ×1·25

**13** ×0·50

**12. YELLOW VETCH** (*Vicia lutea*). This tufted, smooth-leaved annual, common round the shores of the Mediterranean, is rare in Britain and found only very locally on shingle beaches and cliffs, mainly in the south and south-east. Colonies on waste stony and sandy ground near some of our harbours have probably originated from foreign seeds introduced by shipping. The flowers are usually pale yellow, but can also be purplish. The plants are in bloom from June to August and produce black pods with curved beaks.

**13. WALL PEPPER** (*Sedum acre*). Also known as Biting Stonecrop on account of its very acrid juice, this common plant of rocks, walls and sandy ground grows freely inland as well as by the sea. Its finest displays of starry yellow blossoms are to be found on coast dunes and shingle. The matted, fleshy shoots are perennial and evergreen, with closely bracketed leaves, and the flowers are at their best in June and July. The juice inflames the skin and has been used in the treatment of warts.

**14. HOTTENTOT FIG** (*Carpobrotus edulis*). This perennial 'ice-plant', with keeled, fleshy leaves, can be seen hanging in masses on sea cliffs in Cornwall, Devon and the Channel Islands nowadays. It is a South African species which has become naturalised here only where the climate is suitably mild in winter. The large, shining blooms may be either golden or pink. They much resemble the showy Mesembryanthemums which are grown commonly in gardens. The fleshy fruits are edible, but seldom ripen to perfection in this country.

**15. WILD CARROT** (*Daucus carota*). The cushion-shaped flower-heads of this plant make it easy to pick out from its many relatives growing in grassy places. Very often there is a single blackish-purple floret in the midst of the white ones; this looks like a fly and lures insects to the flowers so that they will help in pollination. A seaside variety has very narrow leaves. Cultivated carrots have been developed from this common wild species which has tougher, more stringy tap roots, which are nevertheless edible and rich in vitamin A.

**15** × 0·33

**16. GOLDEN SAMPHIRE** (*Inula crithmoides*). Unrelated to the true samphire, but with similar fleshy leaves, this is a rather tall, succulent plant with golden, aster-like flowers. It grows, often in large clumps, on cliff ledges, shingle beaches and occasionally salt-marshes, chiefly along our south and west coasts. The foliage is glossy and yellowish green, attracting the eye from a distance. Flowering extends from August until late in the autumn. A tough perennial, this species maintains its hold stubbornly.

**17. ROCK SAMPHIRE** (*Crithmum maritimum*). Named after St Peter, the patron saint of fishermen, this cliff plant is common along our south and west coasts, where its spicy fragrance scents the air in summer. Its roots tucked into rock crevices are often more than a yard long. The fleshy leaves are often gathered and pickled in brine or vinegar. The flowers glisten with nectar and attract many small insects on sunny days. An old English name for this plant of the sea-sprayed rocks was 'Crestmarine'.

**17** × 0·20

**18** × 0·25

**19** × 0·50      **20** × 0·50

**18. COMMON SEA LAVENDER** (*Limonium vulgare*). The violet-blue flowers of this species cover many of the vast saltings of our east coast estuaries in July and August. They are much visited by bees, which can be seen flying across the waters to reach them when they are almost covered at high tide. The pointed, tongue-shaped leaves grow in rosettes and are often coloured yellow and red by a rust fungus which attacks them. The blackish, fleshy rootstocks persist for many years in the salt mud.

**19. MATTED SEA LAVENDER** (*Limonium bellidifolium*). Typically a plant of Mediterranean shores, this species is found in Britain only along the East Anglian coast and chiefly near the Wash. There it grows in firm shingle compacted with sand and mud near extreme high-tide level. The basal rosettes of small, daisy-like leaves usually wither as the many-branched, wiry and prostrate flower-heads develop in late summer. The flowers are small, pink and partly encased in conspicuous white papery bracts; they are of two types, each of which is incapable of self-fertilisation.

**20. ROCK SEA LAVENDER** (*Limonium binervosum*). Distinguished from its relatives by the three-veined leaf-stalks, this plant springs mainly from rocky cliff-faces which are within reach of the sea spray. It is most plentiful on the west coast and only patchy elsewhere. In the east of England it can be found on some of the shingle spits bordering salt-marshes near the Wash. The rather slender flower-spikes branch from near the base and the amethyst-coloured blossoms appear in July and August. The dry, papery seed-heads persist until the following summer.

**21. SEA MILKWORT** (*Glaux maritima*). Also known as Black Saltwort, this slender, creeping plant is a member of the primrose family. It forms spreading mats in the grassy parts of salt-marshes all round Britain and may also be found occupying damp crevices in rocks under cliffs. Very much dwarfed plants occur in muddy and sandy hollows of saltings which dry out in the heat of summer; once established they tolerate extreme conditions. The pink flowers appear from June to August.

**21** × 2·00

**22.** **SEA CLUB-RUSH** (*Scirpus maritimus*). Not a true rush, but a member of the sedge family, with three-cornered stems, this is a common plant of shallow, brackish waters. It often forms extensive beds in pools and ditches near the coast and is commonly associated with reeds in these habitats, sometimes growing many miles inland where there are only slight traces of salt in the tidal rivers. Standing three to four feet high, with long, channelled leaves, the plants bear their prominent brown flower-spikes in late summer.

**23.** **SEA HEATH** (*Frankenia laevis*). This small, tough, wiry, mat-forming species has prostrate branches and narrow, heather-like leaves, although it is not a member of the heather family. It grows along sandy and stony fringes of salt-marshes where in July and August its bright pink blossoms expand in profusion on sunny days. The flowers look like minute, fragile, single roses. Belonging to the Mediterranean element in our flora, sea heath reaches its northern limit in Europe on the Norfolk coast.

**24.** **TOWNSEND'S CORD-GRASS** (*Spartina townsendii*). Also known as 'Rice-grass', this plant arose as a fertile hybrid through the crossing of an American and an English species on the south coast of England about a hundred years ago. It has since invaded the soft mudflats of our estuaries very extensively and has also been planted in many places to help reclaim tidal lands. Its matted roots and fast-spreading spear-like shoots hold and build up the level of the mud, soon converting it into firm meadow land. There are infertile forms of this grass and these spread through pieces being broken off and carried to new sites by wind, wave and tide.

**22** × 1·00
**23** × 1·50

**25. STRAWBERRY CLOVER** (*Trifolium fragiferum*). When not in bloom, this can easily be mistaken for the common white Creeping Clover, but from July to September the compact heads of rose-pink flowers and curiously inflated and strawberry-like spherical clusters of seed-vessels make identification easy. Growing almost always on clayey grassland, it has a wide distribution in England and is not confined to the coast, but it is most plentiful on salty clays near estuaries. It is absent in the extreme north.

**26. SEA ASTER** (*Aster tripolium*). This perennial wild blue michaelmas daisy with thick, tongue-shaped leaves grows in muddy salt-marshes which are flooded regularly by the tides. Its flowers appear very late in the summer and are very attractive to bees and butterflies. A variety with yellow, button-like flowers lacking the blue ray-florets has largely replaced the normal form in some places during the last fifty years. In autumn the white, silky fluff of seeding plants is conspicuous round the shores of estuaries.

**27. SHRUBBY SEABLITE** (*Suaeda fruticosa*). Chiefly a plant of Mediterranean shores, this fleshy-leaved shrub is locally plentiful on England's Chesil Beach and on coast shingle in north Norfolk, where it reaches its northern geographical limit. It is sometimes buried by wave-rolled stones in winter storms, but is able to sprout from below and survive. The small greenish-yellow flowers develop in late summer and many of the leaves turn yellow, red or purple in autumn. A smaller annual seablite is common on the wetter salt-flats.

25 × 1·50

**26** × 2·00
**27** × 0·05

**28. SEA WORMWOOD** (*Artemisia maritimum*). This silver-grey, strongly fragrant herb, also known as Sea Southernwood, grows somewhat above the level reached by high tides round the shores of estuaries. It can also be found occasionally on beach shingle and near the bases of cliffs. The finely cut leaves are coated with woolly down to conserve moisture. The golden or reddish flower-heads develop on nodding spikes in late summer. Dried sprigs placed with clothes in wardrobes are said to keep moths away.

**29. MARSH SAMPHIRE** (*Salicornia* spp.). About nine sorts of *Salicornia* grow on our salt-marshes. Most are bright green and fleshy annuals sprouting from bare mud in summer and a few are matted perennials. They are succulent members of the spinach family and are commonly gathered in August and pickled like true samphire by people living on the coast. Known also as 'glassworts', they used to be harvested in great quantities and burnt to produce soda-ash for glass-making. The minute flowers appear in August and September.

**30. YELLOW HORNED POPPY** (*Glaucium flavum*). This grows on many shingle beaches in south and east England. The rosettes of crinkled leaves are frosted with silvery hairs. The butter-yellow and rather large flowers appear all through the summer, each one opening and withering in a day. They have no nectar, but bees and hover-flies visit them for pollen. The long green pods are the 'horns' from which the plant gets its name. The acrid yellow juice is a protection against grazing animals.

**28** $\times$ 0·75

**29** × 0·50

**30** × 0·50

**31** × 0·50

**31. SEA BINDWEED** (*Calystegia soldanella*). Rooting deeply in the sands of our upper beaches and dunes, this sprawling plant has thick, shiny, rounded leaves and very large pink trumpet-shaped flowers appearing from June to September. The blossoms are visited by bumble bees, hawk-moths and certain very small bee-flies. The round, glossy seed-capsules can often be found filled with the chocolate-coloured spores of a parasitic smut fungus. The leaves turn amber yellow as they die down in autumn.

**32.  SEA  CAMPION**  (*Silene maritima*).  A  close  relative  of  the  common
Bladder  Campion  found  by  roadsides,
this  plant  grows  in  great  quantities
on  our  shingle  beaches  all  round
Britain.  It  may  also  be  seen  perched
on  cliff  ledges.  Young  plants  form
spreading  rosettes  which  get  larger
and  cushion-like  later.  The  massed
white  blossoms  are  at  their  best  at
midsummer.  Most  of  the  matted
shoots  wither  after  the  capsules  have
ripened,  but  the  woody  rootstocks
survive  for  several  years  and  often
help  to  stabilise  the  shingle.

**32** × 2·00
**33** × 1·00

**33.  SEA  HOLLY**  (*Eryngium maritimum*).  This  prickly  plant  with  silver-
green  leaves  and  bright  blue,  thistle-
like flowers  used  to  adorn  most  sandy
beaches  and  dunes.  It  still  flourishes
on  our  coastal  nature  reserves,  but
over-picking  by  visitors  has  elimi-
nated  it  from  the  more  popular
holiday  resorts  in  recent  years.  This
is  a  great  pity,  as  there  is  no  more
beautiful  seaside  plant  attracting
bees  and  butterflies  at  the  seaside.
The  bleached  remains  are  still  conspicuous  on  the  windswept  sands  in
winter.  New  leaves  sprout  in  May.

**34. SEASIDE CURLED DOCK**
(*Rumex crispus,* var. *trigranulatus*).
The Curled Dock is a very common
weed of waste ground everywhere.
A robust variety which grows on
sand and shingle along our coasts is
distinguished by having three conspicuous tubercles on its triangular
fruits. The giant flower-spikes are
pale green and up to four feet tall;
later, like the withered leaves, they
become a rich rusty brown, showing
up starkly against the skyline. The
rootstocks persist for several years.

**35. SEA SANDWORT** (*Honckenya
peploides*). A very common plant of
loose sand and shingle on beaches,
growing mainly at and just above the
level reached by the highest tides. It
is a perennial with far-spreading roots
and branches and it helps to consolidate drifting sands. The fleshy,
crowded leaves have a wax-like
polish which prevents them from
damage by blowing sand. The
greenish-white flowers open on
sunny days at intervals through the
summer. Black seeds spilling out of
the capsules often fall into holes dug
by sandhoppers.

**36. CENTAURY** (*Centaurium ery-
thraea*). This member of the gentian
family is usually found growing in
dry, turfy places on coastal dunes
and chalk lands. It is an annual plant,
with flat rosettes of leaves appearing
in autumn and winter. The clear pink,
starry flowers form umbels on stalks
only a few inches high, from early
July to September. They open only
during the day and have a sweet but
delicate perfume like that of the
precious spikenard. Pure white
flowers are common in some places.
Five other sorts of centaury are found
in grassy places along our coast, but
they are all uncommon. *C. pulchellum*
is a slender annual with widely forking
flower-heads. Some others have
densely clustered flowers.

0·16

**35** × 0·33
**36** × 3·00

**37** × 0·75

**38** × 0·33

**39** × 0·50

**37. REST HARROW** (*Ononis repens*). This creeping perennial with sticky hairs on its leaves and pale pink, vetch-like flowers, is widespread in dry, grassy places. It is sometimes plentiful in the hollows of old sand dunes along the coast, but only where some shell-grit is present to supply the lime which this species demands. The foliage has a somewhat resinous scent. The long roots are sugary and have been used as a substitute for licquorice.

**8. TREE MALLOW** (*Lavatera arborea*). This sturdy, tree-like plant, which may reach a height of twelve feet, is a biennial and dies after flowering in its second summer. It grows naturally along our south and west coasts where the winter climate is mild. In Cornwall it is called the 'Ku Tree', because a poultice of the leaves is reckoned to cure styes, for which the local name is 'Ku'. The segmented, cheese-shaped fruits are cupped in three triangular, downy leaves and the seeds produce a mucilage when boiled.

**9. TREE LUPIN** (*Lupinus arboreus*). This Californian shrub with yellow or white flowers, originally planted in gardens, has become widely naturalised on coastal dunes in the south and east of England. It forms dense thickets which collect wind-blown sand and provide welcome shelter for small bird migrants on passage in spring and autumn. The flowers appear from June to September; they are sweetly scented and attract many bees and butterflies. The dead stems are a food for a rich assortment of small fungi in winter.

**0. MARSH MALLOW** (*Althaea officinalis*). This velvety perennial with light grey-green leaves and rose-pink flowers grows in large clumps here and there along the banks of estuaries, mainly in south and east England. It thrives best on clay near slightly brackish waterways and flowers in August. The white roots are strongly mucilaginous and were once much used by herbalists for making a soothing jelly; this also produced the original gluey 'marsh mallow' toffee.

**40** × 1·50

**1. LADY'S BEDSTRAW** (*Galium verum*). Although by no means restricted to the seaside, this yellowest of our bedstraws often grows abundantly on old dunes and sandy wastes along the coast, producing masses of flowers in July and August. It has a strong scent of coumarin, like the Sweet Vernal Grass which gives fragrance to new-mown hay, and for this reason it was used in bedding when people slept on straw. It can also be used as a substitute for rennet in making cheese, and the roots produce a red dye.

**2. MARRAM** (*Ammophila arenaria*) and **PURPLE MARRAM** (*Ammocalamagrostis baltica*). The common marram grass with wiry, tufted leaves and whitish flower-spikes is the main builder of sand dunes along our coast. Its flinty leaves withstand abrasion and catch sand blown up from the beaches so that it collects in hummocks round them. In time, other plants form carpets between the tufts and the sandhills become stabilised. The Purple Marram, with broader leaves and longer, purplish flower-heads, is of hybrid origin.

**42** × 0·10

1·50

43 × 0·20
44 × 1·00

**43. SEA COUCH-GRASS** (*Agro pyron pungens*). This stiff, rather tal blue-green grass is usually the com monest species growing on the bank of estuaries and it fringes the lowe reaches of many tidal rivers. It ca also be seen on old dunes and ston ground near the sea. A close relative the **SAND COUCH** (*A. junceiforme* has larger and fewer spikelets and i usually the first species to become established on the seaward side o marram-crested dunes.

**44. CARLINE THISTLE** (*Carlin vulgaris*). This biennial plant grow commonly on chalk and limeston inland, but it is also a frequen colonist of young dunes which ar rich in limy shell-grit and alkalin minerals from sea salt. It produces pale green, weakly spiny leaves in it first season and these wither whe the flowers develop in the following summer. The leaves are white an cottony underneath. Seeding plants survive in a dried state like everlasting flowers.